MARVELOUS MACHINES

BATTLE STATIONS

WARREN SINGER

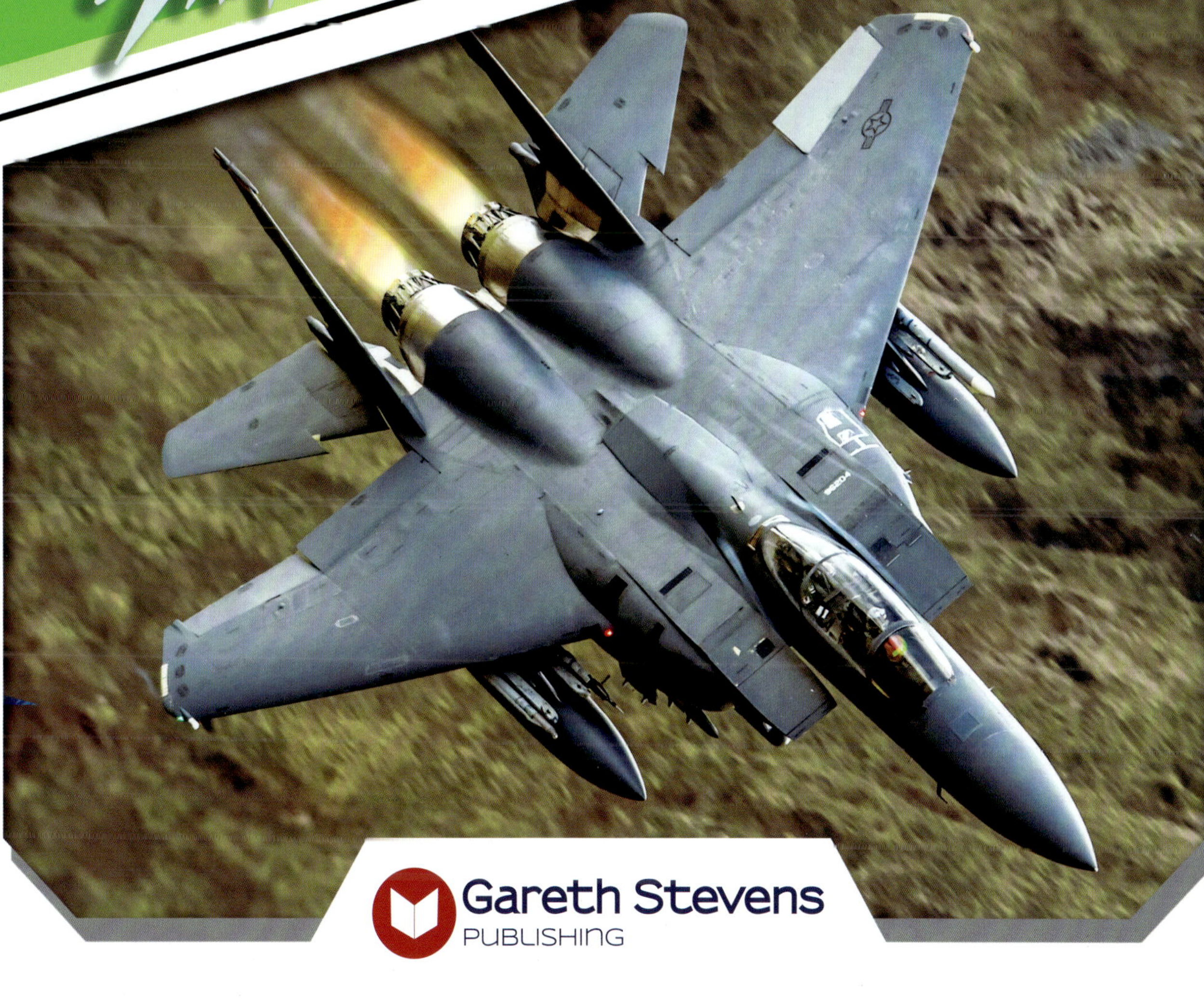

Gareth Stevens PUBLISHING

Please visit our website,
www.garethstevens.com.
For a free color catalog of all
our high-quality books, call
toll free 1-800-542-2595 or
fax 1-877-542-2596.

Cataloging-in-Publication Data
Names: Singer, Warren.
Title: Battle stations / Warren Singer.
Description: Buffalo, NY : Gareth Stevens Publishing, 2027. | Series: Marvelous machines | Includes glossary and index.
Identifiers: ISBN 9781482478136 (pbk.) | ISBN 9781482478143 (library bound) | ISBN 9781482478150 (ebook)
Subjects: LCSH: Military weapons--Juvenile literature. | Military art and science--Technological innovations--Juvenile literature.
Classification: LCC UF500.S564 2027 | DDC 623.4--dc23

Published in 2027 by
Gareth Stevens Publishing
2544 Clinton St.
Buffalo, NY 14224

First published 2025 by Redback Publishing

Author: Warren Singer
Editor: Simone Saba
Designer: Redback Publishing
Original illustrations © Redback Publishing 2025
Originated by Redback Publishing

Printed in China

CPSIA compliance information: Batch #QS27GS
For further information contact Gareth Stevens at 1-800-542-2595.

Find us on

CONTENTS

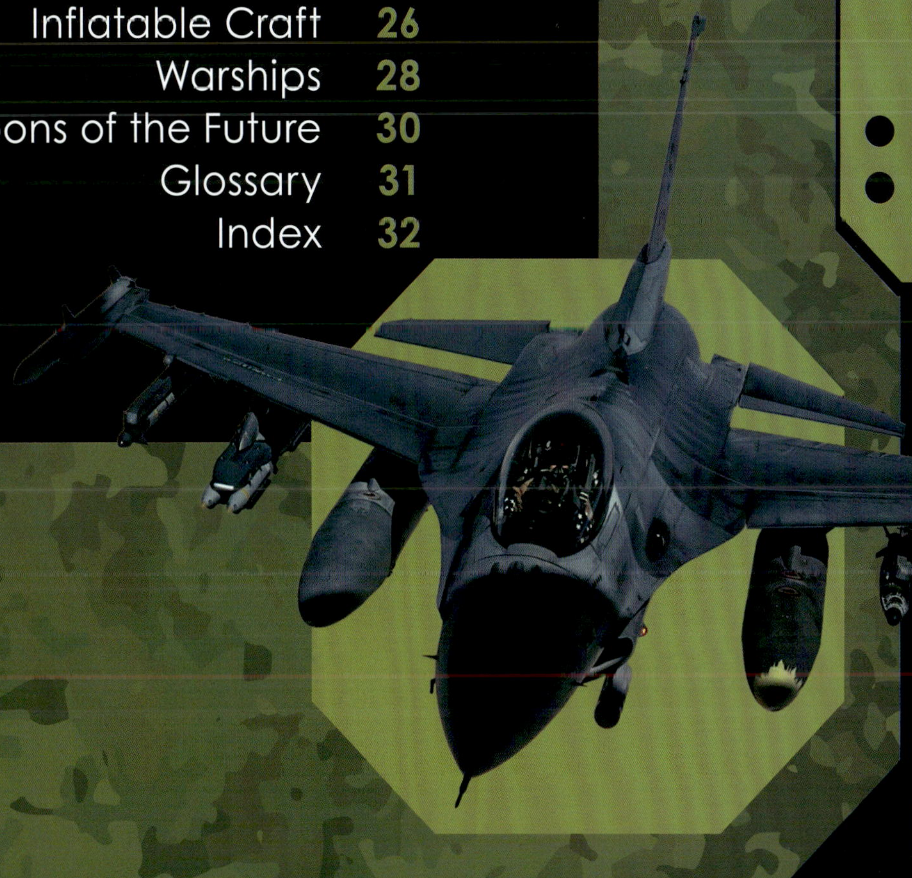

TANKS

Tanks are heavy, and they are made of metal. A metal and rubber strip, called a track, winds around the wheels. The track lets the tank travel over uneven and muddy ground without getting stuck.

Tanks are used in wars to travel close to an enemy. The soldiers inside a tank shoot at targets. They can aim at different targets using the tank turret that spins around on top of the tank.

FAST FACTS

- Over 10 soldiers might be inside a very big tank
- A big tank can weigh as much as 50 small cars

HOWITZERS

Howitzers are large weapons that fire shells at enemy targets. They can hit a target that is over 19 miles (30 km) away. Modern howitzers are made of titanium as well as steel.

Howitzers need to be transported to the site of a battle. They can be towed or carried by trucks, but also lifted by helicopters.

FAST FACTS

- A howitzer shell can travel at over 875 yards (800 m) per second
- The M777 howitzer weighs as much as four small cars

TARGET LOCATORS

Before firing shells at targets, soldiers need to figure out the exact location where they want them to explode. Target locators use lasers to find the exact distance and direction the shell has to travel.

FAST FACTS

- Target locators need to be lightweight
- Laser target locators also use a compass and GPS

MISSILES

A missile is a weapon that is shot at a target, uses fuel to travel through the air, and then explodes when it reaches the target. Missiles can be fired from the ground, a ship, or an aircraft. Guided missiles can find their own way to their target, which might be across an ocean or a whole continent away.

FAST FACTS

- Some missiles have their own jet engines
- The missile's warhead explodes to destroy the target
- Missiles can travel hundreds of miles through the air

BOMB DISPOSAL ROBOTS

Bomb disposal robots can be used to disable live bombs and remove them from an area without the risk of a human being blown up.

The bomb might have been fired or left behind by an enemy but failed to explode when it hit the ground. These bombs could still explode at any time and are a danger to anyone in the area. Bomb disposal robots allow humans to be far away from the bomb while they control the robot, which collects information about the bomb and defuses it.

Soldier wearing bomb disposal gear

FAST FACTS

Robot bomb disposal machines carry:

- X-ray equipment
- Cameras
- Microphones
- Chemical sensors

ARMY TRUCKS

Army trucks come in all shapes and sizes. They often travel in convoys, which is when many trucks are on the road together, one after the other.

Army trucks carry soldiers, weapons, and other supplies. Some of them are amphibious, which means they can travel from land into water, becoming a boat.

FAST FACTS

- Self-driving trucks may soon be used by most large armies

BUSHMASTERS

Bushmasters are heavy vehicles used to transport soldiers into a battle. A Bushmaster has strong metal sides to protect the people inside from attack.

There is a turret on top of Bushmasters. A soldier can use the mounted machine gun by climbing up into the turret.

FAST FACTS

- Bushmasters are made in Australia
- Each Bushmaster can carry up to 10 people
- Bushmasters are air-conditioned

HELICOPTERS

Helicopters can transport soldiers right into a battle zone. A helicopter can land in a small area and take off again very quickly, before an enemy has time to destroy it. Helicopters can assist soldiers on the ground by dropping supplies to them. They are also used for rescues at sea.

FAST FACTS

- Some helicopters can lift over 22 tons (20 mt)
- Most helicopters have between two and seven blades

FIGHTER JETS

Fighter jets are small, fast, and deadly. Fighter pilots train so they can attack and defend, using advanced weapons and flight controls.

Most fighter jets can travel faster than the speed of sound. This results in a loud, booming noise during flight.

FAST FACTS

- Fighter jet pilots train for at least two years
- A fighter jet flies at over 1,243 miles (2,000 km) per hour

AIRCRAFT CARRIERS

Aircraft carriers provide a runway at sea for fighter jets. The jets take off and land over a very short distance along the flight deck.

To stop the jets from ending up in the sea when landing, each one has a hook on its tail that catches strong cables stretched across the runway. These can stop a fighter jet in just seconds!

FAST FACTS

- The largest aircraft carriers carry over 100 fighter jets
- The runway on the flight deck is only about 492 feet (150 m) long

SUPPLY AIRCRAFT

Armed forces need a lot of equipment delivered to them so they can do their jobs. Huge aircraft can carry tanks, helicopters, troops, food, weapons, and more to wherever the men and women in the armed forces are located.

Supply aircraft have wide ramps at the back for loading large and heavy equipment. Sometimes they need to drop supplies from the air to armed forces on the ground.

FAST FACTS

- Supply aircraft can carry over 77 tons (70 mt) of cargo
- The inside layout can change depending on what is being carried

INFLATABLE CRAFT

Armed forces use a rigid-hulled inflatable boat (RHIB) when they need to move around quickly at sea. The boats can move fast, quickly getting up beside a ship or small boat that they need to board or intercept.

Warships carry the inflatable boats and have machines to lower them into the sea and lift them out again.

FAST FACTS

- RHIBs can be over 23 feet (7 m) long
- They can move over the water at 46 miles per hour (40 knots, 74 kph)

WARSHIPS

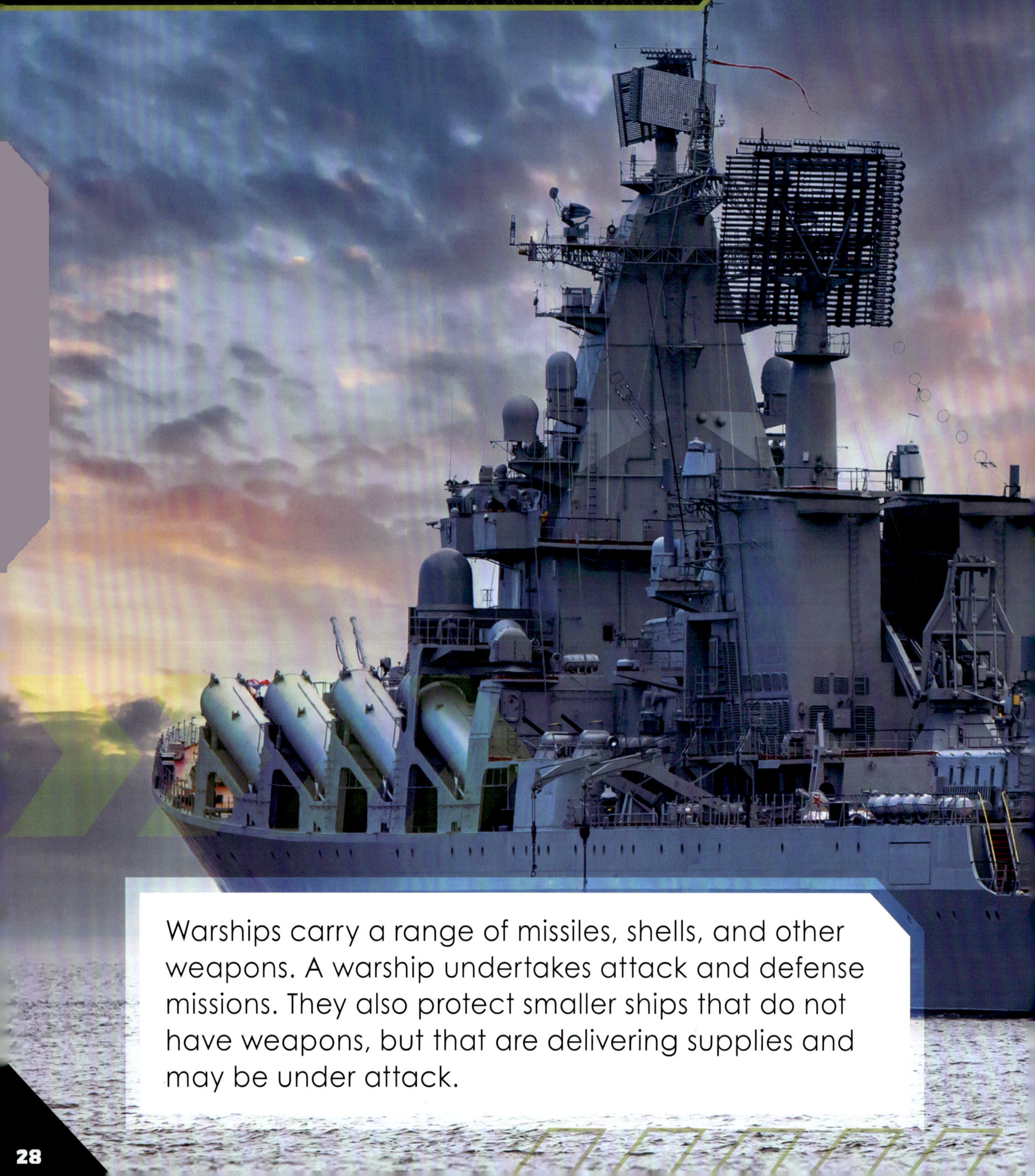

Warships carry a range of missiles, shells, and other weapons. A warship undertakes attack and defense missions. They also protect smaller ships that do not have weapons, but that are delivering supplies and may be under attack.

»FAST FACTS

- The largest warships are over 984 feet (300 m) long
- The best warships are said to be from the United States, China, and Russia

WEAPONS OF THE FUTURE

Designing and making military equipment is a big industry worldwide. What will engineers of the future design for armed forces to use next?

GLOSSARY

amphibious capable of working in water or on land

board go onto a boat or ship

convoy group of ships or trucks traveling together

flight deck part of an aircraft carrier where planes land and take off

GPS Global Positioning System

inflatable able to be filled with air

intercept stop something that is moving

missile weapon that travels to the target with its own fuel

RHIB rigid-hulled inflatable boat

rigid hard

runway road used by an airplane

sensor device used to sense something

shell explosive fired from a gun

titanium metal that is strong and light

track metal and rubber strip around a tank's wheels

troops group of soldiers

turret part on top of a tank where a soldier can sit to fire weapons

warhead explosive part of a missile

X-ray used to see images of what is inside something

INDEX

Acknowledgements

Abbreviations: l—left, r—right, b—bottom, t—top, c—center, m—middle

We would like to thank the following for permission to reproduce photographs: Shutterstock;

Pg5r1 Corona Borealis Studio / Shutterstock.com, pg6c Gal_Rotem / Shutterstock.com, pg7r2 Karolis Kavolelis / Shutterstock.com, pg7r3 Drop of Light / Shutterstock.com, pg7r4 Karolis Kavolelis / Shutterstock.com, pg8c SPC Hilda Clayton, Public domain, via Wikimedia Commons, pg9r1 Cpl. Ned Johnson, Public domain, via Wikimedia Commons, pg9r2 The U.S. Army, Public domain, via Wikimedia Commons, pg9r3 English: Staff Sgt. Cruz G. Sotelo, U.S. Marine Corps, Public domain, via Wikimedia Commons, pg9r4 United States Army Acquisitions Support Center, Public domain, via Wikimedia Commons, pg12c Photo: Graeme Main/MOD, OGL v1.0OGL v1.0, via Wikimedia Commons, pg14c Art Konovalov / Shutterstock.com, pg15r1 PhotoStock10 / Shutterstock.com, pg15r2 Ryan Boedi / Shutterstock.com, pg16c Ryan Fletcher / Shutterstock.com, pg17r2 Ryan Fletcher / Shutterstock.com, pg17r3 Ryan Fletcher / Shutterstock.com, pg17r4 Ryan Fletcher / Shutterstock.com, pg18c Nehemia Gershuni-Aylho www.ngphoto.biz, CC BY-SA 3.0 <https://creativecommons.org/licenses/by-sa/3.0>, via Wikimedia Commons, pg19r3 The Mariner 4291 / Shutterstock.com, pg21r2 The Mariner 4291 / Shutterstock.com, pg23r1 Greg Meland / Shutterstock.com, pg23r2 BeAvPhoto / Shutterstock.com, pg23r4 Mark Van Scyoc / Shutterstock.com, pg25r1 Rix Pix Photography / Shutterstock.com, pg25r3 Fasttailwind / Shutterstock.com, pg25r4 DLeng / Shutterstock.com, pg26c Vytautas Kielaitis / Shutterstock.com, pg27r1 U.S. Navy photo by Mass Communication Specialist 2nd Class Arcenio Gonzalez Jr., Public domain, via Wikimedia Commons, pg27r2 VanderWolf Images / Shutterstock.com, pg27r3 MC3 Robyn Gerstenslager, Public domain, via Wikimedia Commons, pg27r4 U.S. Navy photo by Mass Communication Specialist 3rd Class Robyn Gerstenslager, Public domain, via Wikimedia Commons, pg29r1 Wandering views / Shutterstock.com, pg29r2 Nightman1965 / Shutterstock.com, pg29r3 TheHighestQualityImages / Shutterstock.com, pg29r4 NickolayV / Shutterstock.com